Yellow Umbrella Books are published by Capstone Press
151 Good Counsel Drive, P.O. Box 669, Mankato, Minnesota 56002
www.capstonepress.com

Library of Congress Cataloging-in-Publication Data
Trumbauer, Lisa, 1963–
   Eating well / by Lisa Trumbauer.
   p. cm.
   Summary: Photographs and easy-to-read text introduce the major food groups
and explain the nutritional contributions of each.
   ISBN 0-7368-2937-7 (hardcover)—ISBN 0-7368-2896-6 (softcover)
   1. Nutrition—Juvenile literature. [1. Nutrition.] I. Title.
QP141.T787 2004
613.2—dc21   2003008403

Editorial Credits
Editorial Director: Mary Lindeen
Editor: Jennifer VanVoorst
Photo Researcher: Scott Thoms
Developer: Raindrop Publishing

Photo Credits
Cover: BananaStock; Title Page: DigitalVision; Page 2: Comstock; Page 3: John A.
Rizzo/PhotoDisc; Page 4: BananaStock; Page 5: Comstock; Page 6: Doug Menuez/
PhotoDisc; Page 7: DigitalVision; Page 8: DigitalVision; Page 9: DigitalVision; Page 10:
Nicole Katano/Brand X Pictures; Page 11: Comstock; Page 12: SWP, Incorporated/
Brand X Pictures; Page 13: Comstock; Page 14: Stockbyte; Page 15: BananaStock; Page
16: BananaStock

1 2 3 4 5 6 09 08 07 06 05 04

Eating Well

by Lisa Trumbauer

Consultants: Joan Bushman, MPH, RD,
Member, American Dietetic Association

Yellow Umbrella Books

an imprint of Capstone Press
Mankato, Minnesota

Food

What gives your body the energy to kick a soccer ball or push off on a swing?

Food does! Your body needs different kinds of food to stay healthy.

Grains

Food can be divided into five groups. One of these is the grain group.

Foods in the grain group give you energy. Which of these grains do you like to eat?

Fruits

Another group is the fruit group.
Fruits are packed with vitamins.

Your body needs vitamins to stay healthy. Which of these fruits do you like to eat?

Vegetables

Vegetables are another group.
Vegetables have vitamins, too.
They also have fiber.

Fiber helps your body run smoothly. Which of these vegetables do you like to eat?

Meats, Beans, and Nuts

Meats, beans, and nuts are the fourth group. Peanuts, eggs, and chicken are all part of this group.

These foods help your body grow. Which of these foods do you like to eat?

Dairy Foods

Dairy foods are the last group.
Milk, cheese, and yogurt are
all part of this group.

Dairy foods keep your bones and teeth strong. Which of these foods do you like to eat?

Eating Healthy

You should eat food from each of these food groups every day.

Other foods may taste good,
but they are not healthy to eat.

Eating healthy foods gives your body the energy it needs!

Words to Know/Index

dairy foods—foods that are made from milk; pages 12, 13

fiber—a part of foods such as bread and fruit that passes through the body but is not digested; pages 8, 9

fruit—the fleshy, juicy part of a plant that contains seeds and can be eaten; pages 6, 7

grain—the seed of a cereal plant such as wheat, rice, corn, rye, or barley; foods made from grains include bread, breakfast cereal, rice, and pasta; pages 4, 5

meat—the part of an animal that people eat; beef, chicken, and fish are kinds of meat; page 10

vegetable—the part of a plant that people eat; vegetables can be roots, stems, leaves, flowers, or seeds; pages 8, 9

vitamin—a nutrient that helps keep people healthy; pages 6, 7, 8

Word Count: 214
Early-Intervention Level: 13